A CLASSIC BIBLE CHAPTER

LUKE 15
The Prodigal Son

By

Allen C. Liles

LUKE 15
The Prodigal Son

by

Allen C. Liles
Liles Communications, LLC

Published By
Positive Imaging, LLC
bill@positive-imaging.com

All Rights Reserved

No part of this publication may be reproduced in whole or in part, or stored in a retrieval system, or transmitted in any form or by any means, electronic, mechanical, printing, photocopying, recording or otherwise without written permission from the publisher, except for the inclusion of brief quotations in a review. For information regarding permission, contact the publisher.

Copyright   2021   Allen C. Liles

ISBN: 9781951776701

This book is dedicated to my dear wife
and partner in ministry
Jan Carmen Liles

(1941-2017) RIP

Contents

Introduction		1
Preparation For Studying Luke 15 The Prodigal Son		5
Biblical Text		9
Luke 1-7	The Parable of the Lost Sheep	9
Luke 8-10	The Parable of the Lost Coin	10
Luke 11-32	The Parable of the Lost Son	10
Jesus Decides to Use Parables		**15**
Prodigal Son Stories		**23**
The Prodigal Daughter		23
The Prodigal Father		34
The Prodigal Mother		39
The Prodigal Brother		44
The Prodigal Sister		52
The Prodigal Child		62
The Prodigal Son's Brother Tells All		**71**
The Prodigal Son Sits Down for an Interview		**75**
The Prodigal Son's Father Explains Everything		**79**
Understanding The Prodigal In Your Life		**83**
The Twelve Gifts of the Prodigal Son Parable		**89**

A Final Thought/Why We Are All Prodigals	95
About the Author	97
Books by Allen C. Liles	99

INTRODUCTION

This is a book about leaving one's family, squandering money on riotous living and then receiving redemption. It also presents one of the greatest examples of unconditional forgiveness ever recorded in human history. It is the famous parable of "The Prodigal Son", found in Luke 15: (14-31) in the Holy Bible.

Jesus Christ was a master teacher. He taught in many ways: parables (interesting stories with a meaningful point), precepts (short and profound statements of Truth), miracles (visible results of divine action) and general observations (containing sacred wisdom). He shared his revolutionary message with large crowds, like at the Sermon on the Mount and in the Temple at Jerusalem. He also engaged in one-on-one instruction, such as with the Samaritan woman at the well in his discourse on the "living water".

Many of Jesus' teachings were misunderstood, even by his closest followers. The Disciples had trouble deciphering their LORD's deep messaging at "The Last Supper". Who was this "Holy Comforter" that God was sending as His replacement? Where exactly was Jesus going and what did He mean by "preparing mansions" for them? The Master spent his three years of public ministry enlightening and informing the world of His time. However, only a tiny percentage of these teachings were understood by the masses. His themes of hope and correct spiritual behavior were designed to bless humankind. But most of His listeners were practical people with limited abilities to grasp the hidden meanings. Thankfully, much of Jesus' inspired teaching did survive in the Gospel writings of Matthew, Mark, Luke and especially John.

One of Jesus' most important messages involved forgiveness and redemption for "the lost". In the Classic Bible Chapter Luke 15, the Master presents three key parables about the "lost" being "found". These parables are "The Lost Sheep", "The Lost Coin" and "The Prodigal Son." Of this trio, "The Prodigal Son" ranks as the most famous and often quoted. In truth, every human being has been a "prodigal" or known someone with prodigal behavior. Most everyone has engaged in wasteful and reckless spending and foolish behavior. There are no perfect human beings. We all need forgiveness at some point in our lives. In this parable, Jesus reiterates how bad decisions can cause us to experience loss. Once we embark on a path of awakening and recovery, a return to wholeness becomes possible. Extending and receiving forgiveness is always a crucial aspect of that journey. The worldwide programs of Alcoholics Anonymous, Al-Anon Family Groups and Narcotics Anonymous represent visible examples of how the "Prodigal Son" parable has relevancy today. Jesus' teachings were meant to offer hope for recovery through a spiritual awakening. The parables in Luke 15 focus on the theme that nothing of value is lost forever. The father of the Prodigal Son modeled unconditional love. For those recovering from addiction and behavior issues, receiving forgiveness from those they harmed may not be easy. Considerable emotional, physical and spiritual damage can be caused by dysfunctional behavior, destructive addictions and irresponsible actions.

What brings people to the place where they are ready to both receive and practice forgiveness? We live in an egocentric, sarcastic and cynical world. Most everyone can benefit from exploring the healing aspects of forgiveness. Of course, you and I have already received personal forgiveness through God's Grace. But what about those human beings we have harmed with our words and actions? How do they find forgiveness for us? Perhaps most crucial of all, how do we forgive ourselves? Read and consider again the parable of "The

Introduction

Prodigal Son". Meditate on its relevance in your life today. Perhaps somewhere in that famous teaching by Jesus, you will find the answers you seek.

Allen C. Liles
Temple, TX

PREPARATION FOR STUDYING
LUKE 15

OPENING PRAYER:

LORD, please help me learn how to forgive. Open my consciousness to the benefits of releasing the past. Help me to let go all hurts and resentments. Give me true understanding and acceptance as I wipe clean the slate of unforgiveness. Provide me with generosity of heart and mind. Let me grant a full pardon to those who knowingly or unknowingly harmed me. May I see everyone surrounded by the Light of God. This is a new day. I am a new person. Assist me in releasing all negative memories. Thank you, God. Amen.

MEDITATION

Find a quiet and familiar place where you can remain undisturbed for a minimum of 15 minutes. Sit with both feet flat on the floor. Place your hands in your lap with the palms turned upward. Now take a deep breath. Breathe in through your nose, until your lungs are filled with air. Hold that breath and count silently to yourself 1-2-3-4-5. Now open your mouth and push your breath out, again counting 1-2-3-4-5. Take on more deep breath and repeat the same process.

Now read these words: "Dear God, I come to you now in the silence of this sacred moment. I ask for your help in completing the decision to forgive. I seek your strength in accepting this sacred opportunity. I knock at Heaven's door and ask for the spiritual tools necessary to forgive. Let me empty out all hurtful memories. This is a moment for healing. Assist me in understanding the benefits of forgiveness for everyone. Above all, help me to find forgiveness myself. I did the best that I could at the time. Thank you, God."

Close your eyes and sit in the silence for five full minutes. Listen for the still, small voice of the Holy Spirit that lives within you. Perhaps you may sense a divine Presence at the core of your being. Have no expectations as you remain fully quiet and attentive. Know that the Holy Spirit is at work on your behalf. Treasure this time in the peace and quiet, whatever the outcome. Embrace the serenity that comes in the quietness. God wants this time alone with you. Consider coming back each day or night to experience again this unity with your Creator.

PRAYER OF THANKSGIVING

Lord, thank You for this time alone with you. I feel your divine Presence. I know you want me to live in a state of forgiveness. Please put your blessing on my efforts to find a forgiving attitude toward everyone. I praise your ways. I am leaning on your understanding to move me forward on the spiritual Path. I am so grateful. Thank you, thank you, thank you God. Amen and amen.

LUKE 15

BIBLICAL TEXT

Luke 15: 1-7   The Parable of The Lost Sheep

15:1---Now the tax collectors and sinners were all gathered around to hear Jesus.

15:2—But the Pharisees and the teachers of the law muttered, "This man welcomes sinners and eats with them."

15:3—Then Jesus told this parable:

15:4—"Suppose one of you has a hundred sheep and loses one of them. Doesn't he leave the ninety-nine in the open country and go after the lost sheep until he finds it?

15:5—And when he finds it, he puts it on his shoulders

15:6—and goes home. Then he calls his friends and neighbors together and says, "Rejoice with me. I have found my lost sheep."

15:7—I tell you that in the same way there will be more rejoicing in heaven over one sinner who repents than over ninety-nine righteous persons who do not need to repent."

Luke 15: 8-10   The Parable of the Lost Coin

15: 8—Or suppose a woman has ten silver coins and loses one. Doesn't she light a lamp, sweep the house and search carefully until she finds it?

15: 9—And when she finds it, she calls her friends and neighbors together and says, 'Rejoice with me; I have found my lost coin."

15: 10—And in the same way, I tell you, there is rejoicing in the presence of the angels of God over one sinner who repents.

Luke 15:11-32   The Parable of the Lost Son

15: 11—Jesus continued: "There was a man who had two sons.

15: 12—The younger one said to his father, "Father, give me my share of the estate." So he divided his property between them.

15: 13—Not long after that, the younger son got together all he had, set off for a distant country and there squandered his wealth in wild living.

15:14—After he had spent everything, there was a severe famine in that whole country, and he began to be in need.

15:15—So he went and hired himself out to a citizen of that country, who sent him into the fields to feed pigs.

15:16—He longed to fill his stomach with the pods that the pigs were eating, but no one gave him anything.

15:17—When he came to his senses, he said: How many of my father's hired servants have food to spare and I am starving to death!

15:18—I will set out and go back to my father and say to him: Father, I have sinned against heaven and against you.

15: 19—I am no longer worthy to be called your son: make me like one of your hired servants.

15:20—So he got up and went to his father. But while he was still a long way off, his father saw him and was filled with compassion for him; he ran to his son, threw his arms around him and kissed him.

Biblical Texts

15: 21—"The son said to him, "Father, I have sinned against heaven and against you. I am no longer worthy to be called your son."

15:22-"But his father said to his servants, "Quick! Bring the best robe and put it on him. Put a ring on his finger and sandals on his feet.

15: 23—Bring the fatted calf and kill it. Let's have a feast and celebrate.

15: 24—For this son of mine was dead and is alive again; he was lost and is found." So they began to celebrate.

15:25—Meanwhile, the older son was in the field. When he came near the house, he heard music and dancing.

15:26—So he called one of the servants and asked what was going on.

15:27—"Your brother has come home," he replied, "and your father has killed the fattened calf because he has him back safe and sound."

15:28—The older brother became angry and refused to go in. So his father went out and pleaded with him.

15:29—But he answered his father, "Look! All these years I've been slaving for you and never disobeyed your orders. Yet you never gave me

Luke 15: The Prodigal Son

even a young goat so I could celebrate with my friends.

15:30—But when this son of yours who has squandered your property with prostitutes comes home, you kill the fatted calf for him!"

15:31—"My son," the father said, "you are always with me, and everything I have is yours,

15-32—But we had to celebrate and be glad, because this brother of yours was dead and is alive again, he was lost and is found."

JESUS DECIDES TO USE PARABLES

Following is a fantasy conversation involving Jesus Christ and the Apostles Peter, John and Thomas prior to The Sermon on the Mount, scheduled for the following day.

PETER: *"Well, boss, is your talk ready for tomorrow? I hear they are expecting a big crowd at the mountain. Are you set? Do you have some new stuff prepared?"*

JESUS: *"Actually, I'm in a bind. I have too much material for just one sermon. I am worried their eyes may start glazing over before we're done."*

JOHN: *"What sort of things are you planning to lay on them? How long will your speech go?*

JESUS: *"Frankly, I don't think I can finish it all in one day. It is really a lot of material. I have enough stuff for two, maybe three full days."*

THOMAS: *"Uh-oh. I don't know if the people are up for that. Their attention span, especially for the goatherders and fishermen, is not all that great.*

Jesus Decides To Use Parables

PETER: *"Is there any way you can cut it?"*

JESUS: *"I don't think so. Most of the material is being channeled from God. I don't think the Holy Father likes being edited."*

THOMAS: *"Don't look at me. I hesitate to question God. He already thinks that I am a doubter. Let me ask you: Is it all good material?*

JESUS: *"It is all incredibly relevant, maybe some of the wisest observations I've ever made. The problem is that the copy machine and the printing press won't be invented for many centuries. The information will be coming so fast that taking notes will be next to impossible. I doubt if the people will be able to remember it all."*

JOHN: *"How do you plan to handle it?"*

JESUS: *"I am thinking about assigning each section to a specific Disciple. That person would commit his or her portion to memory. Then, after the speech is done, we can all get back together and try to sort everything out."*

THOMAS: *"I don't know, chief. That sounds like it might lack some consistency. With all due respect, some of the Disciples are not all that swift. Your talking points might get garbled."*

JESUS: *"I do have one other idea that might make a difference."*

Luke 15: The Prodigal Son

PETER: *"Let's hear it. I don't care for the memorization thing."*

JESUS: *"I'm thinking about using something easy to illustrate my points. It's called "parables".*

THOMAS: *"Para-whatibles?"*

JESUS: *"A parable is kind of a fictional ministory with a spiritual point at the end. People relate more easily to everyday real-life stories. I think they might also remember them better."*

PETER: *"I don't get it. Give me an example."*

JESUS: *"I know you enjoy your wine after a hard day on the Sea of Galilee. You like your wine fresh. If you had a couple of old wineskins lying around, you would not pour the new wine into the old stuff. Would you?*

PETER: *"Of course not. You need new wineskins for new wine. How is that a para-able or whatever you are calling it?"*

JESUS : *"You made my point. You would not pour the new wine into the old wineskins. If you are changing and becoming a new person, you need to get rid of your old habits. You wouldn't want to mix the new you with the old you. Do you see?"*

JOHN: *"That seems like an easy example. Do you have any more of these stories you can share with us?"*

JESUS: *"Actually, I have about forty- five or so of these little parables that I could lay on the crowd."*

THOMAS: *"Whoa! don't know about that. I understand these folks. They are an impatient group. You always get a lot of murmuring if you don't get right to the point. It's just the way they are. You might want to consider hitting them with two or three quick stories, but certainly no more than that."*

JESUS: *"What would I do with the rest of my time? I want to teach these good souls about a better way to live, with a deeper love for God and each other in their hearts."*

PETER: *"There is nothing wrong with that approach. Do you know any good jokes? People always appreciate a laugh."*

JESUS: *"Joke telling is just not my style. My time with the people is so limited. God is giving me some terrific information that I need to get across as soon as possible."*

JOHN: *"I heard an interesting story a few days ago. It was about a father and his two sons. It seems that the youngest kid got restless and wanted to leave the family farm for the big city.*

Luke 15: The Prodigal Son

He also asked for his inheritance. The old man did not like the idea. He figured his son would blow the money. But he wanted to be a good dad. So, he gave the wild child his share of the family fortune and let him scram."

THOMAS: *"So what happened?"*

JOHN: *"Just about what you would expect. The kid fell in with the wrong crowd. He was even living next door to a bunch of prostitutes. People said he was their best customer."*

THOMAS: *"I will bet the money did not last very long."*

JOHN: *"That is absolutely correct. Plus, the kid was getting drunk before noon every day. He was a real mess."*

PETER: *"What happened when the money ran out?"*

JOHN: *"He ended up broke. There was a famine going on and he needed to make some money. So, the kid hired out to a pig farmer on the edge of town. His job was to feed and slop the hogs every day."*

THOMAS: *"I'll bet he did not like that after being raised with money."*

JOHN: *"You are correct, sir! It did not take our wayward lad long to figure out his old man's servants were living better than him."*

PETER: *"So he was not completely stupid. What did he do then? Hightail it back home?"*

JOHN: *"You got it. He planned to grovel at his father's feet and ask for a servant's job. Anything was better than slopping the hogs."*

THOMAS: *"So what happened when he got back home. Did the old man tell him to take a hike?"*

JOHN: *"No, just the opposite. The father saw him approaching from a distance. According to the story, the dad ran out to greet him. When the son tried to grovel and ask for a servant's job, the father would not hear of it. He sent somebody back to the farm to fetch a fancy robe. He also told his people to kill the fatted calf and arrange for a feast in honor of the wayward son."*

THOMAS: *"That's hard to believe. What did the other son think about all of that? He could not have been happy. When the wild brother split for sin city, he probably had to shoulder all of his duties"*

JOHN: *"You are spot on, Tommy. When he heard they were having a party in his brother's honor, he saw red. He went straight to the*

Luke 15: The Prodigal Son

father and complained. Pretty loudly, or so the story goes."

PETER: *"Did the old man back down? The brother had a point, you know. It doesn't seem fair that he did the right thing and the wild child gets honored with a feast. A fatted calf? That is big-time celebrating. I would be upset too."*

JOHN: *"The father did not change his mind. He stood his ground. He just told the angry son that his brother had been lost and was now found. That was cause for celebration. He was back at home."*

JESUS: *"I love the story. It personifies forgiveness. I think it is perfect for a parable. I even have a name for it."*

PETER: *"What's that, boss?*

JESUS: *"I will call it "The Prodigal Son".*

THOMAS: *"That's certainly better than "My Son the Hog Slopper."*

PETER: *"You got that right."*

PRODIGAL SON STORIES

THE PRODIGAL DAUGHTER

Her high school years were a never-ending nightmare for Ashleigh Radcliff. Each day unfolded with new disappointments, humiliation, and rejection. Ashleigh's anger built accordingly. Resentments mounted daily. Her only path to survival consisted of wall-building. Those cast outside of her steel barrier included family, teachers, acquaintances, institutions and God. There were few exceptions. She placed a deep moat filled with alligators and poisonous snakes in front of her wall, just in case someone might dare venture in. The only human beings gaining rare passage included other females that aroused her sexual interest. These young women were usually beautiful, popular and strangely attracted to Ash's profound weirdness.

Every high school boy was excluded from consideration. An acutely bad case of acne scarred Ashleigh's face. That helped keep the male gender far away. She had zero dates with anyone from the beginning of her freshman year to graduation day four years later. Attending senior prom was unthinkable, although she did consider asking one of the school's female cheerleaders. She wisely decided not to test their tentative relationship. On prom night, Ashleigh huddled in her bedroom watching lesbian porn. Besides her parents, Ash's primary nemesis was her older brother. Jason Radcliffe was 13 months older than his younger sister. Marijuana and heavy metal music were his only interests. Jason had discovered weed at a rock concert on his 14th birthday. It was a committed love affair from first toke. Of course, his high school journey became an afterthought. After a string of academic failures, he officially left school at the mid-point of his senior year. The incident that triggered his departure involved a fight at the high school. Jason had stiffed one of the football team's offensive linemen on a minor dug deal. The hefty 250-pound tackle rendered Jason unconscious with one right cross. The dazed teenager woke up 20 minutes later in an assistant principal's office. It was the last day he set foot inside that high school.

Jason took out his frustrations on his younger sister, who was having her own challenges. Ashleigh's facial disfiguration because of the acne made for an easy target. Jason's pet name for his sister was "Ugly". It was "Hey, Ugly" this and "Hey, Ug" that. Neither of her parents called a halt to the abuse. In her angry mind, they were excusing Jason's unacceptable behavior. It was part of a family pattern that rendered Ashleigh even more vulnerable and undefended. She blamed her dad more than the mom for not protecting her. By this time, the mother had detached from the family dysfunction. She embraced the neighborhood ladies' Happy Hour that specialized in box white wine and vodka gimlets. The drinking became an afternoon ritual. It usually followed a quick set of tennis or some mall shopping. Ashleigh had once regarded her father as the only other sane person in the family. As such, she looked to him for relief from her brother's cruel taunts and mom's budding alcoholism. However. the clueless dad seemed more intent on his corporate career than saving his only daughter from the mounting torment. Ash's animosity toward her father eventually exceeded the fury directed at the mother and brother. The white-hot hate for the entire family group became her motivator for escape.

Jason's antics demanded what attention anyone could spare. Little was done about his drug use, lack of school attendance, multiple car crashes and general flaunting of acceptable social behavior. Of course, official trouble with law enforcement soon materialized. He was arrested for selling a large bag of pot to an undercover agent. The father paid $2000 to a criminal defense attorney and his son was spared any jail time. He did receive a three-year unadjudicated probated sentence and a stern lecture from the hard-eyed judge. Jason spent his time in court arguing with the judge, who described him as a "medium-size drug dealer". His defense attorney kept advising him to "shut up and be respectful."

Jason did neither and exited the courtroom surly as ever.

Meanwhile, Ashleigh was becoming angrier and more even detached from the family. After graduation from high school, she immediately split for the main state university in Austin. It was more than 200 miles away and a safe distance from the turmoil. There was one major surprise. Despite her severe acne, she decided to go through the sorority Rush Week. Besides her scarred face, Ash's social skills were questionable at best. Surprisingly, she managed to secure a pledge from an off-brand sorority specializing in rejects from major female Greek groups like Zeta, Kappa, and Pi Phi. However, Ashleigh was quickly booted from the dubious sorority. She was caught in a flagrant sex tryst with one of her "pledge sisters". Both girls were ousted and escorted from the sorority house. Ashleigh moved alone into an off-campus efficiency apartment and spent the next four years focusing on her communications studies.

She was a brilliant student and graduated in the top 5% of her class. Ash's IQ tests were just below genius level. The entire family had once taken an intelligence evaluation. Her mother, father, and brother all had the same IQ score—128, twelve points below the genius threshold. Ashleigh came in at 138, a full 10 points ahead of everyone else in the family. "By God, I always knew that I was the smartest one in the family", she told herself

Luke 15: The Prodigal Son

with glee. The IQ test seemed to bolster her always shaky self-esteem.

After college, Ashleigh briefly moved back home. She discovered that nothing had changed with her parents and brother. If anything, things were worse. Her mom and dad were openly snarling at each other. Divorce was being discussed. Jason had just completed a major court-ordered 84-day stint in drug rehab. As a part of that process, the entire family was required to attend a therapy session with a noted psychiatrist. After the raucous get-together, the doctor requested a release from the family to use a tape of the session for teaching purposes. His class was titled "A Highly Dysfunctional Family".

After her college graduation with a degree in Media Communications, Ash only paused long enough to collect a few personal things at home. She then split for California without looking back. In her resentful mind, there was no reason whatsoever to remain physically near her family. Ashleigh never once thanked her dad for the $100,000 he had invested in her communications degree. Subsequent letters written by the family to her in California by either parent were trashed without reading. She rarely responded to their texts or calls. Of course, she never once inquired about her brother Jason. The estrangement did not bother him. He was busy drugging, clubbing and promoting the fourth or fifth incarnation of his heavy metal band. Ashleigh's ties with her family had long been frayed. When the university campus emptied out for Thanksgiving, Christmas or Spring Break, she almost never went back home. The lack of contact with family felt like a blessing. She knew her dad's corporate career had gone all right and Mom finally sobered up through AA. But she had zero interest in any of their lives. When Ash crossed the state line on I-40 heading west for California, she finally felt free forever from the family stigma.

When she arrived in the Golden State, Ash decided to drive north towards the Bay Area. She chose the scenic route on the Pacific Coast Highway 1. Ashleigh was blown away by the natural beauty she encountered. One of her college profs had relocated to the Cupertino area, near San Jose. Armed with his telephone number, she called him. The professor was gracious and invited her to stay at his place during the relocation process. The prof also told Ashleigh of a nearby Silicon Valley start-up that was hiring. During her first full week in California, she found the company's HR department and filed an application for employment. The actual head of HR called the following day and made an appointment to interview her. Within a few days, Ash reported for work in the three-person Communications Department. It was love at first sight for the Texas girl. She loved everything about the high-tech world. The heady excitement of wild and unbridled growth infected her psyche from the beginning. She received the first stock option exactly one year after arriving at the company. It was amazing that a single piece of paper could turn into $250,000 overnight. Within three years, Ashleigh had made her first million. By the time she celebrated her 30th birthday, she had a net worth of five million dollars. Meanwhile, any attempt to contact their daughter by her family back in Texas went mostly unanswered. When asked by her mom for a contact number, she had supplied the main corporate office number. The transplanted Californian also stayed off any social media that might provide a family connection. As far as Ash was concerned, they all lived on a distant planet. In her brain, it was a safe distance from her own galaxy.

The transplanted Texan fell in love with her boss at the company just before her 35th birthday. The pair had known each other for many years. However, the two had never been never romantically involved until recently. The professional relationship and friendship burst into passionate love without warning. Within six months, Mary Ellen had proposed marriage and Ashleigh accepted without any hesitancy. They honeymooned at a Thai beach resort before settling in at a palatial mansion two miles from company headquarters.

"You are quite a package," Mary Ellen whispered before she had asked for Ashleigh's hand in marriage. "You are beautiful, built like a brick outhouse, super intelligent and the best lover ever." It was all true. The dreadful acne had long since vanished. Ashleigh's figure had become voluptuous without any cosmetic surgery or implants. She had a wild and hot streak that always captivated her many female lovers. She was indeed a "package".

Ash had never experienced true love in this form. Her Texas family had certainly never met any emotional needs. She and Mary Ellen were forced to part ways at the corporation because of a rule that partners or married couples were not allowed to work together. However, Mary Ellen transferred to the International Division, so that had introduced an interesting new element into their relationship. Ash loved to hear about her husband's exotic travels. She was lounging at home alone one evening when the TV news was interrupted by a special bulletin. A passenger jet with several hundred people aboard had disappeared over the Indian Ocean. There was no trace of the wreckage. Ash's heart leaped into her throat. She knew Mary Ellen was traveling somewhere in the vicinity. Logging on to her partner's home computer, she pulled up M. E.'s itinerary for the current trip. One of the flight numbers matched that of the missing plane. Ashleigh went into immediate shock. Within an hour someone at the company had called to confirm the unsettling news. The caller tried to offer some hope, but Ashleigh's heart told her the unthinkable had happened.

Luke 15: The Prodigal Son

The next few weeks were the most horrendous of Ashleigh's life. Of course, she flew to Southeast Asia the next day and waited with other relatives for any news of the missing plane and possible survivors. Nothing was forthcoming. A desperate search of the ocean came up empty. It was a mystery for the aviation ages. Ash finally retreated to Northern California, still in total shock. It was a full three months before she had recovered enough to hold a memorial service for Mary Ellen. She also delayed returning to work, opting instead to sleep up to 18 hours a day. Becoming a widow before the age of 40 was proving difficult. She felt bereaved, stunned and hopeless. Her parents had tried to call, but finally resorted to sending a printed sympathy card. Ashleigh did not respond. One day, just as she awakened from a lengthy nap, a FedEx truck pulled up in front of the mansion. The driver had lucked out in catching Ashleigh in a rare moment of consciousness. He presented her with a slim package. It contained a brief letter from her mother. Ash immediately thought of tossing it unread into the trash. But, for some reason, she decided to give it a read. The letter contained these words:

"Dear Ashleigh,
We are so sorry to hear about Mary Ellen's tragic and unexpected passing. Although we never had the pleasure of meeting her, I am sure she was a wonderful person. Our thoughts and prayers are with you during this sad

time. I wish I had some better news from Texas, but things have been bad here too. Both your father and brother are in the hospital. Your brother has never taken very good care of himself. Now he is coping with COPD and various other respiratory problems. I am hoping he can come home from the hospital next week, but I do not know if he will ever be well again. He was evicted from his apartment three months ago and his latest girlfriend wanted no part of being homeless. Jason has been living with us for the past few weeks. I am also sad to report that your father was diagnosed this week with a glioma or Stage 4 brain cancer. The doctors gave him 12 to 18 months. Evidently surgery is not an option. Your dad seemed to take the news better than I did. As for me, my lupus is acting up, but I'm the healthy one right now. I wish I had better news, but we know you have your own issues. You are always in our thoughts and prayers, even after all these years. We will always love you. You are still our little girl.
With love, Mom.

Ashleigh stared at the shaky handwriting for at least sixty seconds. Then she crumpled up the letter and threw it into the closest wastebasket. Afterwards, she went straight to bed and fell asleep almost immediately. Within a few minutes, Ash was deep into a riveting dream that featured her lost love. In the dream, Mary Ellen was standing at the foot of her bed. She was dressed in a flowing white robe with a lovely purple sash. In a shocked voice, Ashleigh asked: "What are you doing here?" M. E. did not speak but she reached into the pocket of her robe and fetched something. It was the crumpled letter from Ashleigh's mother. In the dream, Mary Ellen carefully smoothed out the bunched-up letter. Then, she looked at Ashleigh and spoke in a beautiful and clear voice: "Listen to me, my dearest one. Here is what I have learned since arriving in God's Kingdom. You never have enough rainbows in your human life. Forgiveness and acceptance are the secrets to a happy existence. Grudges corrode the soul. Your parents did the best they could at the time. Your brother always carried his own demons from several unsettled past lives. He never had a chance in this incarnation. You were given this family for a reason. You are here to demonstrate forgiveness, compassion and understanding. It is your soul lesson. Your family needs you at home. Yes, it's hard to let go of the past, but the time has come. I hope you will consider it. Do not worry about their reaction. They will welcome you home with open arms. They love you, Ash, and so do I. Please do this favor for them and also for me. Give everyone another chance, my sweetheart. Go home."

Then, Mary Ellen's image disappeared into the ethers. Ashleigh's eyes popped open. They were filled with tears. She strolled into the kitchen and was surprised to see the previously crumbled letter, lying face up on the counter. It had been carefully smoothed out. Beneath the letter was the FedEx package from yesterday. Ashleigh picked up the larger envelope and noticed that it contained another wrapped document. It was an open round-trip airline ticket from California to Texas and return. There was a post-it sticker on the outside of the ticket. In her mother's shaky handwriting, the note read:

"We are hoping that you come back to us someday. We will always love you, our darling daughter. (signed) Your family"

Maybe it was indeed time for her to go home

THE PRODIGAL FATHER

Women loved every part of Ron Trotter, some parts more than others. Whether they were young, middle aged or elderly, it did not matter. The female gender could not get enough of Big Ron and his dreamy blue eyes and uncommon physical endowments. He was 12 when the seduction of his 17-year-old babysitter was

Luke 15: The Prodigal Son

consummated. At 16, he twice impregnated his twenty-something cocktail waitress girlfriend. Ron was not yet 18 when he became a prospective father again through a steamy relationship with the daughter of his town's police chief. The gruff law enforcement officer gave Ron two choices: marry his 17-year-old daughter or join the military and leave town. Ron chose the United States Navy. He loved the excitement of the seafaring life. Ron managed to have a different girl in every port, and there were lots of ports during his four years of service. Before he was discharged, Ron thought briefly of making the Navy a career. But he had a line on an interesting job with a mid-size police department as a rookie patrolman. The military life and law enforcement seemed like a natural fit. Ron aced the exam and graduated #1 in his class at the police academy.

It did not take Ron long to figure out that a form-fitting police officer's uniform was an add-on feature to his already fatal attractiveness to females—and males as well. He easily turned away potential men suitors, but the women were another story. His nightly dance card was always full and sometimes overflowing. Ron became a highly proficient "player", able to string along five or six women at the same time. He craved variety. Age, professional status, ethnicity or cultural background were no impediment to his insatiable sexual appetite. By the time Ron turned 30, his conquests numbered in the high hundreds. Of course, the amoral lothario had not escaped unscathed. He was forced to deal with a few sexually transmitted diseases along the way. However, nothing slowed him down. There were more than a few uncomfortable moments with jealous husbands. irate fathers, incensed boyfriends and even protective sons of his many partners. When that happened, it helped to play the police officer card. Ron knew that he had broken dozens of hearts along the way. The emotional part of his constant dallying, he tried not to think about. The women will get over it, he reassured himself. Then, Ron met Deborah. Everything changed. She was intelligent, exquisitely beautiful and far above his pay grade socially. Her father was a self-made and well-connected billionaire. Ron had met Deborah while working security at a charity auction. As was his way, he openly flirted with the former debutante and wealthy heiress. Of course, Deb proved just as vulnerable to Ron's handsomeness and masculinity as any less rich conquest. The pair became intimate in less than a week of their first meeting. However, Deb's innate intelligence kicked in immediately. She sensed Ron was indeed an active "player" with a roving eye. How could any woman possibly "tame" this epitome of infidelity? Easy, she thought to herself—marriage, money and babies. Most men want a secure home, sufficient cash in the bank and a loving family around them, Deborah told herself.

Her plan worked almost perfectly, at least for a while. The couple eloped to Las Vegas and were married at a wedding chapel on the Strip. Deb's family did not attend, but she quickly smoothed over that key relationship. She became pregnant and the couple produced a beautiful baby daughter before celebrating their first wedding anniversary. Ron did miss baby Lorraine's birth. He was "shacked up" at a motel downtown with a female detective from the Homicide Division. Deborah accepted his sincere apology with the thought: "Maybe one baby isn't enough". Believing that premise, she produced four more equally darling baby daughters over the next six years. Ron soon found himself surrounded by half-a-dozen attractive, charming and attention-craving females. They all doted on him. He was overwhelmed by their affectionate love and acceptance. As Deborah had hoped, it profoundly changed his life.

There were still a couple of slips now and then. However, for the most part, the six beautiful and active women at home were more than a handful. They kept Ron totally occupied. Sooner than Deborah could have imagined, Ron's wandering eyes became blind to other women. However, his obsessive ways were now fully trained on guarding his family harem at all costs. Beginning with his wife, Ron became paranoid about any other male that might dare encroach upon his happiness. His greatest fears centered around his daughters Lorraine, Margaret, Jennifer, Betsy and (most of all) the young Priscilla whom he dubbed "Pumpkin" or "Punkin" for short. Ron became more questioning than the FBI when teenage boys began venturing on the scene. He even put together a probing questionnaire that each young man had to complete or be banished from consideration. All potential suitors were run through the police data base for any red flags. More than one young man told Ron to "shove it". However, most complied because of the girls' individual beauty and voluptuous figures.

Ron was especially suspicious of one "Punkin" boyfriend. Mikey Dolan was six years older than Priscilla, who had just turned 17. The age difference was already a problem for Ron. In addition, there was something seemed strangely familiar about Mikey. For one thing, he looked exactly like the son Ron never had. The teenager was tall for his age and extremely muscular. Mikey's blue eyes mirrored his own. When Ron checked the boy's Q and A form, his heart tore upward into his throat. Arnie had listed his father as "deceased" but noted that the mother was a retired homicide detective with the local police department. Ron realized the boy's possible lineage almost at once. Maybe Mikey Dolan was indeed the son he never had. Except now, the young stud was also a potential interloper threatening his most prized possession. The Prodigal Father had a giant problem he could have never imagined. He quickly turned to his wife Deborah for advice and comfort. She just smiled and shook her head. The past had caught up with the Prodigal Father.

THE PRODIGAL MOTHER

Raynoma Johnson was born in the Motor City and grew up attending a famous black church, led by a well-known and dynamic minster. The pastor's daughter, who sang in the church choir, would someday become a famous diva and the Queen of Rock and Roll. Raynoma was an alto in the choir and loved the spiritual vibes that burst through the ceiling of the old sanctuary. Her entire family (mother, father, four sisters and two brothers) all went to church religiously, no pun intended. They all loved the spirituality that flowed up to the rafters from the African American congregation and back down again. Raynoma had a deep and personal relationship with a benevolent God that she loved and cherished. Her human father, Raymond Lee Johnson, had landed a job on the assembly line at the Ford factory in Dearborn after World War II. He stayed with the automaker until his retirement in the late 1960s. Raynoma's mother, Pearlie Mae Johnson. clerked for many years at a black-owned drug store off West Grand Boulevard until it was torched in the 1967 riots. Both of Raynoma's brothers had long careers at the downtown post office and each retired with a government pension. Her four sisters all married military men, three of whom saw service in the Vietnam War. All of Ray's sisters eventually relocated to Southern California. Back in 1961, her mom told Raynoma about one of her customers who had just started a new record company in Detroit. She suggested that Ray drop by his offices and leave an application for employment. Pearlie Mae knew the man was adding office staff. Raynoma went by the new offices and spoke with the owner himself. They clicked immediately. Within a week, she began work as a general secretary for the company. Ray was the ninth person hired by the trailblazing firm that would someday change the direction of the music industry forever.

Raynoma loved her job. It was intoxicating, being in the middle of a creative group of writers, musicians, producers, and artists. She also adored the assorted characters that functioned on the fringes of the business. One day, she met an outside publicist and promotions man that worked with black radio stations to feature the company's top performers. B. B. Brown was 28, four years older than Raynoma. He was a non-stop charmer that could sell anything to anybody. B. B. sold himself to the young secretary and they soon married. It was just two years later that their twin boys B. B. II and Barry Gordy Brown were born. Raynoma quit the job she loved and focused on being a full-time Mama. The founder at the record company discreetly presented Raynoma with a $100,000 cashier's check on her last day at the

Luke 15: The Prodigal Son

company. Everything worked out fine until 1972. Ray's husband had started his own PR firm and was flourishing with several lucrative management contracts. The family relocated to a large house in Grosse Pointe formerly owned by a Ford vice-president. The family easily adapted to the suburban lifestyle.

Then one day, she received an unexpected call from her former boss at the record company. He had decided to move his headquarters to Los Angeles. "We'll be closer to the action." He told her. "I want you to come back to work as our office manager," adding, "I need someone around me that I can trust. Besides, I believe you and the family would like Southern California. No more Michigan winters. You and your family will have fun in the sun. I will start you at $75 K a year. You won't get that in Detroit City, no way, no how. I will also throw in some stock options and a company car. Think it over, Ray. I would like your answer by the end of the week."

After Raynoma hung up the telephone, she wondered if it had all been a dream. When B. B. showed up in the late afternoon, she asked if they could sit down for a talk. "Are you pregnant again?" he asked, "I hope it's not another set of twins." The tart answer seemed unexpected and hurtful. She knew B. B. loved the boys. When Raynoma informed her husband of the generous offer, he grimaced. "That guy," he said in referring to his wife's old boss, "I wouldn't trust him as far as I could throw him and that's not very far. He always had his eye on you, Ray. I'll bet he wants to get you out in L. A., all to himself."

Raynoma was startled by her husband's negative reaction. He had never once shown any animosity towards her old boss, much less jealousy. She dropped any further discussion of the idea. At the end of the week, she telephoned the record label's office and left a gracious message for the owner. She regretfully declined the job offer.

Another week went by. Then, her ex-boss called again. "I want to sweeten the offer, Ray," he said. "I will make you a vice president of administration for the entire company. Your base salary will be $100,000 per year, plus a $50,000 bonus if we hit our profit goals. That should be a sure thing. Look, I know B. B. is probably against this opportunity for you. But this could be your ticket to the big time. Our company is going to the moon. We already have four records by our top artists in Billboard's Top 10. This is your chance, Ray. I may even help B. B. get a client or two out here if he will agree to move with you. Do this thing, not only for me but for your entire family. They would love it out there. Think about and call me next week with your final answer. A "yes" would really mean a lot to me."

Luke 15: The Prodigal Son

Raynoma felt conflicted. Things were made more difficult by both of her parents' situation. Her father had retired from Ford and was interested in moving to Florida. Ray's mother no longer worked and moving to warmer weather sounded good to her. After dinner one evening, Raynoma asked B. B. and the boys if they could have a formal family meeting. She wanted to give her sons a voice in the decision. Ray presented the new job offer to the family. However, B. B. was still against the idea and the twin boys also reacted negatively. "No way," B. B. II said, "I've got a new girlfriend and I really like her." "I'm just starting football here," Barry added, "I don't want any part of moving away." B. B. just stood up and said, "You already know how I feel. I'm going out for an ice cream. Does anybody want to come with?" Both of the boys jumped up and shouted "Absolutely!" and "Count Me in!", respectively. Within a few seconds, Raynoma was sitting in her living room alone.

She closed her eyes. An idea popped into her mind: "I should ask God what I should do." She took a deep breath and prayed: "Father, which way should I go? What should I do? The family wants no part of this opportunity. I guess I can't be selfish and think just about myself. Please tell me what to do, sweet LORD."

Everything was quiet for a while. Then, she heard a still small voice from deep within her soul. It answered Raynoma's question in a clear and unambiguous tone. The voice spoke only four words. "Always follow the music," it told her. And she did. Eventually, everyone in the family thanked the Prodigal Mother for moving them to a fabulous new life in The Golden State.

THE PRODIGAL BROTHER

Antonio and Tomas Rodriguez were identical twins. Tony was the oldest by 15 minutes. Tommy was a quarter hour younger and two ounces lighter. Both were the same length, 21 ½ inches. Antonio came into the world screaming. Tomas silently appeared with a wry smile. Each had a visible trace of fine dark hair. Tony resembled Angelica, his beautiful Hispanic mother. Tommy also favored Angie slightly more than he did dad Carlos. One of the nurses in the maternity section of the East Angeles hospital made a prophetic comment to the family: "It will be a real challenge for you and other people to tell them apart." No one could possibly know the absolute truth of that off-hand prediction.

As they grew up, the boys' personalities could not have been more different. Tony was the typical older brother (even by only a quarter of an hour). He was respectful, responsible, and dutiful. Tommy was the exact opposite, always in trouble and often scolded. It did not take the younger brother long before he realized the advantages of their similar appearances. He started to dismiss accusations of wrongdoing, saying "That wasn't me. It must have been my brother Tony." Of course, no one could ever stay mad at Antonio for very long. Even if Tommy's deflections had been true (which they never were), Tony's sweet and gracious personality could smooth over any ruffled feathers. Even teachers and school administrators were often confused. Tommy even convinced his identical twin to serve a few detentions for him. Tony loved his younger brother too much to refuse. By the time they had graduated from high school, most people understood the drastic behavioral differences between the pair. However, strangers unaware of their identical appearance could wind up confused and puzzled. The boys' themselves sometimes participated in the joke. They would sometimes show up on blind dates pretending to be the other brother. It made for some interesting times until they explained themselves. Most often, the girls involved were far from amused. When the boys ventured out socially together, people often stopped and gawked at their perfect likenesses. Since they got along so well with each together, the brothers were flattered by the attention.

After high school, a big change occurred for each brother. Antonio had loved being a part of the school's ROTC military group. The discipline and team aspect of the unit appealed to his sense of order. It seemed quite natural for him to enlist in the U. S. Air Force. Antonio easily passed the physical and mental requirements and was soon off to basic training at Lackland AFB in San Antonio. Meanwhile, Tomas decided to leave California. In the vast Hispanic community, he felt like a tiny minnow in a sea of voracious whales and sharks. Tommy bought a United States map and sat for days pondering the huge and diverse country state by state. After considerable study, he decided on a radical move to cold country. To his parents knowledge, Tomas had never seen snow before. He had stuck a pin on the city of Bloomington, Minnesota. His dad Carlos and mother Angelica were blindsided by Tommy's decision. He also asked them for his share of the family savings account and they reluctantly agreed. The parents were not happy losing both sons at the same time. However, they nodded a tepid semi-approval and gave Tommy a nearly six-figure cashier's check for his journey. Instead of using the money to purchase a solid car for the trip, Tomas opted for an old Volkswagen Beetle. The speedometer had been rolled back numerous times, but it did boast a relatively new transmission and recycled motor. He had the vintage VW repainted bright orange and christened it "Cal" for "Caliente" ("Hot"). To Tommy, his tiny car was definitely "hot stuff". He only checked briefly in the rearview mirror as his parents stood in the driveway waving goodbye. He got out on the freeway, sailed through Flagstaff on I-40 and then sped across New Mexico until intersecting with

I-35 in Kansas. After that, the little bug chugged due north until it hit the East-West 435 loop that circled Minneapolis. He took the Mall of America exit and began looking for the cheapest Bloomington motel he could find. On his first night in Minnesota, a group of "Vikings" gang bangers spotted the bright orange VW parked in the motel parking lot. They approached Tommy after noticing his California license plate. Finding out he was an actual East L. A. resident earned him instant street cred. They did not even seem disappointed after learning that he had no gang affiliation. The "Vikings" invited him to a party in one of the motel "suites". He gladly accepted the offer. By the weekend, he was a new "pledge" of the budding gang, which was just beginning to earn its niche with law enforcement in the Twin Cities. At his first formal meeting, the "pledge captain" passed out the written requirements for gang membership. Tomas was given a list of five crimes. He was told that to earn his official gang status, he had to commit at least two of the five crimes mentioned. His choices included (1) steal a car and dump it within 24 hours; (2) vandalize a school or church; (3) shoplift at a Mall of America retail store; (4) beat someone up without putting them in the hospital or (5) rob a Superamerica or Holiday convenience store. Most prospective new members chose vandalization and shoplifting. A few were into car-theft, so that was a natural choice for them. The two most dangerous crimes were physically attacking someone or robbing a 24-hour store with security cameras and possibly an armed clerk or customer who might intervene. More than a few attempts at beating someone up had not ended well. Several "pledges" had been injured while attacking old and seemingly helpless victims. One potential gang member lost an eye to a 90-something lady's knitting needle. Another grabbed an elderly man and was surprised when the old dude turned out to be a retired professional wrestler. The "pledge" ended up in the ER with a fractured elbow and three broken ribs. Tommy opted for the safer crimes of vandalization and shoplifting. Unfortunately, both backfired. He was busy marking up a church one night when he was spotted by a husky neighborhood security guard. He was able to get away, but the guard had punched him in the mouth. Tommy lost three teeth. Since the Vikings gang membership did not include a dental plan, the trip to a licensed dentist cut into his parental stake by several hundred dollars. His shoplifting attempt at a Mall of America store did not fare much better. Besides the risk of security cameras, the retail outlets were now employing undercover agents. A statuesque Swedish woman at a mall clothing store wrapped him in an immediate headlock when he tried to steal a name-brand belt. The Bloomington police released Tommy because of his clean record in California and his new residency in Minnesota. But the arrest put him into the state "system". It was not an auspicious beginning for the would-be gang mem-

Luke 15: The Prodigal Son

ber. He finally did put some gang markings on the backside of a small church without cameras or security. He was also able to steal one running shoe from a Mall of America store during a noisy protest in one of the courtyard areas. The disruption distracted the store employees long enough for Tommy to make his swipe. Although his criminal forays had been rather tame, he was officially accepted as a "Vikings" gang member. Several members of the crew then accompanied their newest recruit to his required "tatting" at a nearby tattoo parlor. The marking itself was the standard "Viking" head, complete with beard. helmet and spear. The artwork was lifted directly from the local NFL team. Some gang members objected, thinking they might be mistaken for football fans instead of gang members. But the tattoo parlor owner had NFL season tickets, so the choice was allowed to stand.

The gang life was new to Tommy, but he tried to get with its flow. Although never a big drug user other than pot, he tried to increase his weed use while avoiding the harder stuff. He was mostly a beer drinker anyway, so he just piled on a few extra cervezas. None of the gang challenged his moderate use of drugs and alcohol. The sex life aspect of the gang gave him the most trouble. Women flooded through their "clubhouse", always looking for a taste of the wild side. Tomas' good lucks and sweet manner earned him at least three or four serious propositions every week. He mostly begged off, but his reluctance to engage in rampant sex caused some consternation among his fellow Vikings. "What's the matter with you, bro?" he was asked more than once. When one of the gang members directly questioned his manhood, Tommy felt pressured. He began a brief affair with "Maria", one of the group's most devoted followers. She was compliant, but sensed his reluctance. Maria quickly dropped Tommy for a rowdier gang member recently released from the Hennepin County jail.

Tommy did use some of the "Prodigal Son" money from his parents to purchase an older motorcycle. However, he never cared much for the bike, preferring his beloved flame-colored VW instead. He continued displaying a tepid response to the gang's criminal activity. He always seemed occupied when their more dangerous plans went down. He only fired his standard gang issue .45 caliber handgun once, at a metal trash can. The kick from the gun surprised him. He dropped the weapon and it fired again upon hitting the ground. The bullet narrowly missed hitting Tommy in the ankle. The young man felt like he was on probation with the gang. They knew he wasn't a "snitch" or "rat", so nobody physically threatened him. But the transplant from East L. A. would never be considered for officer status in the gang structure. He was only a half-hearted gang banger at best.

Luke 15: The Prodigal Son

Tommy was sitting in the "clubhouse" one day watching television. There was a national story about an Air Force helicopter pilot on a rescue mission in the Gulf of Mexico. An oil rig had blown up and a dozen or so workers were tossed into the shark-infested waters. The young pilot had heroically responded and managed to rescue everyone. He was being interviewed on network news about the incident. One of Tommy's fellow gang members shouted, "Hey, bro. That's you on TV!" There was his twin brother Antonio, explaining that the dangerous rescue mission was just standard operating procedure. Tony seemed modest and self-effacing about his heroism. Tomas felt impressed and proud. That night in bed, he lay awake thinking about Tony and his exemplary accomplishment. The next day, Tommy called his parents. "I'm coming home," he told them. "I saw my bro on TV yesterday. That's the kind of life I want for myself. If they will have me, I'm going to join the Air Force too. I'll start driving back to California later today. I'm coming home. That is, if you all will have me." There was silence on the other end of the call. But Tommy could tell someone was crying. Then, his mom said in a grateful vice: "Of course, we'll have you. Your dad and I love you. Please come home to us."

Tommy never went by the Vikings club house to say goodbye. He had miles to go before he slept.

THE PRODIGAL SISTER

The five Rogers sisters (from the Kansas City suburb of Overland Park, Kansas) were all smart, beautiful and talented. They were also divinely blessed with attractive and endearing personalities. In alphabetical and birth order, they were Adele, Alana, Amelie, Astrid and Avanka. Each was an original. Adele was the most statuesque and commanding of the sisters. Alana had a mischievous and playful manner. Amelie presented a dark-haired French look. She was the seductive and amorous one. Without any effort on her part, "Ammy" attracted male admirers from every age group. Astrid was 100% Swedish in appearance and boasted a surprising practicality. Avanka's model-like features appealed to every camera. Her radiant and perfect complexion was envied by all. Taken together, the Rogers' girls were a formidable collection of feminine beauty, uncommon intelligence and radically different personas.

They all possessed extraordinary singing voices. Altos, contraltos, sopranos and even a bass (Avanka) emerged to form a musical blend both pure and distinctive. They first began singing at church, but their sheer talent soon expanded to other venues. By their high school years, the "Rogers Five" was famous in the Missouri/Kansas state line area. Then, the girls caught the eye of a Branson talent scout. Their first booking in the Ozark vacation capitol was a rousing success. The girls soon found themselves signed to a Nashville record contract. Adele was 22, Alana 20, Amelie 19, Astrid 18 and Annabelle 16 when fame selected them. Within a few months, the girls became show business marvels. Their first album stirred up millions of downloads and sales. They appeared on countless national TV shows. There was a worldwide discovery of their unique singing abilities, beauty and winning personalities. An incredible future loomed before the still humble girls. Blue skies and green lights lay before them.

Their parents, Charles and Rosemary Rogers, were not totally surprised. Most moms and dads, who are themselves outstanding, know when their children are also blessed. Charles served as the senior music minister at the largest Baptist church in the Kansas City area. Rosemary was personal assistant to the chairman of the world's premier greeting card company. They both gloried in the emergence of their offspring as talented and blessed. The Rogers were a happy, fulfilled and deeply grateful family.

The first scent of potential trouble came to the Rogers Five's personal manager. Henry R. (Buck) Masters was a Nashville veteran and show business legend. In nearly half a century of artist management, Buck had seen it all. His daddy, "Red" Masters, had known every one of

The Grand Old Opry's original founders and stars. He also was friends with the legendary studio musicians that could make a break a hit record. Both Buck and Red (now deceased) knew where every corpse in Music City was buried and who they were buried with. Buck usually kept his cool, no matter how outlandish the star behavior became. The Rogers Five were an absolute joy compared to some of the messes he had cleaned up over the years. He became an official "grandpappy" to each one of the lovely sisters.

When the unexpected call came from one of his girls, Buck stayed silent and just listened. The veteran manager thought he had heard everything. However, this revelation was a true stunner. One of the sweet Rogers girls had just emptied her heart out to "Grandpappy". She waited now for his response. Buck cleared his throat three times before speaking. He was the definition of "crusty", but the tears in his voice were wet with emotion. "Well, honey, I don't know," he managed. "Have you shared this secret with anyone else?" he asked, already anticipating the answer.

"No, you're the only one," the girl replied to Buck's surprise, "I can't talk to mom, dad or any of my sisters. They might have me committed on the spot. I feel bad about messing everybody up. But I am not confused about what I must do. Right now, I'm living a lie. I cannot continue doing that for the rest of my life. I'm not a girl, Grandpappy. I may have been born as one, but it was a mistake. I need to correct it before things go on any longer. Do you have any advice?"

Several thoughts entered Buck's mind. He had many heard many insane comments from booze and drug-addled entertainers. But the person sharing this revelation did not come across as "crazy". She just seemed worried about what her family might think. That did not strike Buck Masters as insane at all. In fact, he detected a huge portion of compassion for the turmoil she was about to unleash on her family—and the world at large. Most of all, Buck felt protective toward Avanka, the youngest Rogers sister.

"Are you sure about this, honey?" he asked. "This is a pretty big step. How long have you felt this way? Did something happen that brought it to a head right now? Can you enlighten me?"

"I've known for a long time," she replied. "I just denied it. For our household, this is big-time radical thinking. I'm positive that my family will think I'm nuts. It may destroy our relationship forever. I'm also sure it will be the end for the "Rogers Five". It certainly will become the "Rogers Four". Don't you agree?"

"Well, I don't know how your sisters will react and neither do you," Buck answered. "Were you planning on telling anybody else in the next day or two? More importantly, how do you see this all playing out? Are you going to have sex change surgery anytime soon?"

Buck sort of hoped for a negative response to his last question. However, Avanka did not hesitate.

"Yes," she replied, "I already have a doctor picked out. He is probably the best person around for this sort of thing."

"When are you thinking about doing it?", Buck asked in a more urgent tone of voice.

"I have an appointment in two weeks," Avanka responded. "I need to tell my parents and sisters before I go in. Something might leak and I don't want them to get blindsided. Mom could have a heart attack. She already has some problems in that area. With my dad, he might stroke out. I am expecting some anger from the other girls. A couple of them may never speak to me again."

"Do they suspect anything?" Buck Masters inquired.

"Absolutely not. I haven't told anyone, even Astrid. She and I are probably the closest. I have not said a word to anyone in the family. You are the first".

"How about in the "trans" community? This is too big a deal not to tell someone. Have you confided this to anybody else that may have gone through something like this? Be honest with me, sweetie. SOMEBODY outside of you must know about it. Think. What about the surgeon?"

"At this point, I used a fake name to make the appointment. I will need to straighten that out when I go in person."

Buck's brain was finally beginning to process the shocking news. He tried to react in a rational and supportive manner. He wanted to continue being in the loop about Avanka's plans. A completely negative reaction might sever their communication.

"My first inclination would be to hold two separate meetings," he said, "Ordinarily, I would recommend you tell Charles and Rosemary before your sisters. However, my gut is saying the girls need to know first. You have more than a family relationship with them. You are professionally tied together. No doubt about it, this will affect their music careers. You owe them some professional courtesy. So, your first meeting should be with your sisters as a group. I would not do it individually. Do it with all four at the same time. Am I making any sense at all?"

"I was thinking the same thing," Avanka responded in a relieved voice. "I need to get straight with them first, even before mom and dad. But I am not expecting any high fives from anybody. I know better than that. However, I hope they can find some compassion in their hearts for me."

"Is there a love interest involved?" Buck inquired. "Yes and no," Avanka replied. "I do have a friendship with someone, but it has not evolved into something more."

"Is he or she aware of your plans?" he probed, hoping for a negative answer.

"No," Avanka affirmed, "Only two people outside of the surgeon know anything. That is me and now you. If something leaked, everything would blow up within five minutes. I know that, believe me."

"Still," Buck advised, "I would have your meeting with the sisters ASAP. Secrets are hard to keep. The sooner, the better."

Avanka followed the advice of Grandpappy. She called each sister individually and asked if they could convene at Adele's new condo the next day. Everyone said yes. Curiosity fueled the quick acceptance by everyone. Formal meetings among the girls were rare and usually initiated by the adults.

Luke 15: The Prodigal Son

Adele quickly put together a light lunch for everyone. Once that was completed, she turned to Avanka and said, "It's your meeting, hon, what's up? You're too young and innocent to get pregnant, so spill it."

The youngest Rogers sister cleared her throat. "Well," she said, "I've got something to share. It's been on my heart for a long time."

"Is it about you being gay?" Alana asked with a grin.

"Are you finally coming out of the closet?", Astrid chimed in, "It's about time. Everyone already knows it."

"I'm betting it is a little more than that," Adele offered, "Am I right?"

Amelie arched her eyebrows.

"Are you about to become a boy on us, 'Vank"? she offered.

Everyone focused their respective eyes on the youngest Rogers girl.

Avanka drew in a deep breath and waited a few seconds before answering Amelie's question.

"Yes, I am, "she said quietly.

There was a collective intake of air with every girl.

Finally, Alana spoke.

"Well, then, there, now," Alana whispered in a low voice.

"Would you care to elaborate?" Astrid inserted. "Are you going to have sex change surgery?"

"Yes," Avanka nodded.

"When are you planning to do this?" Adele solicited.

"Pretty soon," Avanka responded. "Maybe in the next three months or so. It takes time to get something like this scheduled."

"What would you like from us?" Astrid asked.

"Well, I honestly don't know. Acceptance maybe. Understanding, for sure. Feedback?"

"We always knew why you sang bass," Alana smiled.

"We are still the Rogers Five," Adele injected, "No matter what sex we may be at the time."

Avanka began to cry. Somebody passed her a box of tissue.

Luke 15: The Prodigal Son

"This is unbelievable," she said through the tears.

"Look, 'Vank," Astrid said as she draped her arms over her sister's shoulder. "Here is the deal: people are just people. Forget about everything else. Put aside the rest, all of it. God created each one if us in Her image and likeness. He didn't design us to be judged by the color of our skin, sexual preference or how we vote. We are human beings, walking the earth as best we can. I love each one of you unconditionally. I believe that God operates in the same way. Nothing we can ever say, do or be ever causes the Holy Spirit to back away from us. I'll be quiet now. That is my sermon for the day."

"Amen and amen," Adele clapped,

"That says it for me," Alana added. Astrid and Amelie nodded their assent.

"Again, what do you want from us?"

"Support with mom and dad?" she finally offered.

"Oh, they already had things figured out a long time ago," Alana smiled. "Anything else? If not, I'm still hungry. Let's go and get a pizza."

THE PRODIGAL CHILD

When Richard Henry Fillmore was born, his vital statistics buzzed around the hospital. Nurses were amazed by his length (26 ½ inches) and weight (16 pounds six ounces). One of the docs said: "We better let the football recruiters know about this kid now". His father, William Robert (Billy Bob) Fillmore, was barely six feet tall and a wiry 160 pounds. Richard Henry's mother Louise was a normal size person as well, standing five feet six inches and weighing 140 pounds. In the early stages of her pregnancy, Louise thought that she might be carrying twins. But the ultrasounds confirmed just one child, but a biggie. Since this was her first, she was unsure about what to expect.

After a couple of years, Richard Henry was still big for his age. Conventional and medical wisdom said you could double a person's height at age two and get the final height. As he blew out the candles on his second birthday cake, Louise measured her son. He was already 40 inches tall. At that rate, he would top out at six feet eight inches. In his pre-school class, Richard Henry's size was matched only by one other child, the son of an NFL defensive lineman. When the young boy entered elementary school, he was subject to some teasing by other children. That ended when he knocked one third grader unconscious with a single punch He also gave a fourth grader some chipped teeth.

To the other kids that did not engage in bullying or hurtful comments, Richard Henry was a quiet and polite classmate. Other boys were always inviting him to participate in team sports. However, he never seemed interested. Instead, the youngster showed an immediate artistic side. Sitting down one day at the elementary school piano, he just began playing with surprising ability. His mother Louise immediately signed him up for piano lessons. After less than a year, the teacher called to say his talents already exceeded her own. She suggested Richard Henry be enrolled in the closest Arts Magnet school as soon as possible.

The impressive young man measured six feet four inches tall by the seventh grade. He also weighed nearly 200 pounds. Several middle and high school football coaches scheduled exploratory visits to the Fillmore household. Receiving no encouragement, they finally left him alone. In the eighth grade, Richard Henry enrolled in a "Modern Dance" class at the Arts Magnet. He was an immediate sensation. He asked for and received private ballet lessons. His teachers were startled by his immediate talent for that elegant form of dance. Word began to circulate about his unique and natural gifts.

Louise was proud of her son's artistic bent. However, dad Billy Bob was not so sure. In fact, he was more than a little embarrassed. He had expected a linebacker but instead had received a ballet dancer capable of beautiful pirouettes.

His fellow service technicians at the car dealership did most of their teasing behind his back. However, when anybody mentioned Richard Henry's expanding notoriety, he did not hesitate to defend his son's talent for the arts. Still, it came as a total shock one evening at the family dinner table when Richard Henry made an unusual announcement.

"I want to sign up for the Golden Gloves," He said quietly. Billy Bob dropped his knife and fork. Louise did not trust her ears. She asked for a repeat. "I want to box," the teenager confirmed. "I will need your permission. I hope you will give it to me."

Billy Bob shook his head. "Son, with your size, you would have to fight in the heavyweight division. You could really get hurt. There are some big boys in that class."

"That is what I like," Richard Henry nodded, "I want to fight somebody my own size. That appeals to me."

"Absolutely not," Louise said in a final tone of authority. "I won't have my son getting hit in the face by some stranger."

"I've been hit in the face with words ever since I can remember," their son replied. "I want the chance to hit back—legally. It's just a boxing match."

It took some convincing, but his parents finally agreed. Richard Henry completed the paperwork, they signed off and the young man became an official entrant in the area's Golden Glove competition. Everyone was amazed by this unexpected development. Billy Bob's friends in the service department were impressed. Nearly 20 people from the dealership bought tickets to the matches. Louise opted not to attend. She did not want to witness the expected carnage. She told anyone who would listen: "My child does not have a mean bone in his body."

Billy Bob accompanied his son to the weigh-in. Richard Henry measured exactly six feet, eight inches in height. The scales totaled 237 pounds, mostly congregated around his waist. His legs were spindly and white. Richard's long trunks appeared ill-fitting. In fact, he had them on backwards. He was nearly a foot taller than his opponent. However, neither Billy Bob or Richard Henry had ever seen anyone with such muscular arms and torso. The young black man smiled through several gold teeth as he was introduced to the Golden Gloves officials. He looked up at the young white boy with narrowed, but not unfriendly eyes. There was almost a scent of pity directed toward his latest "victim". After the weigh in, someone told Billy Bob that the muscle-bound fighter had won by a knockout in every fight of his short career. Most came in the first round. On the way home, the dad tried to convince the son not to go through with the fight.

"Nobody will think less of you," he told Richard Henry. "You have never been in the ring with anyone. This guy is almost a professional. He could really hurt you."

"Don't worry, Dad," his son had said. "I'm a foot taller than him. It's only three rounds. This will give me someone to vent my anger against. What can possibly go wrong? I can handle it. He actually seems like a nice guy."

With the fight only a few days out, Billy Bob took his son by a local fight gym for a "lesson". He explained to the owner that Richard Henry might need some help with his non-existent pugilistic technique. "Who is he matched up with?" the gym owner asked. When Billy Bob offered the opponent's name, the other man burst out laughing. However, his demeanor instantly turned serious. "You can't let your boy get into the ring with him," he said, "That guy is a stone-cold killer. I believe he will be the heavyweight champ before he's done. He's that good. Your kid won't last the first minute of the first round."

Richard Henry just smiled. He would lose too much face if he backed out now. For the first time, the young man was receiving positive attention at school. There were no more "sissy boy" comments about his ballet or piano lessons. No, he had to go through with it.

There was a big crowd gathered for the opening of the Golden Gloves competition. The heavyweight matches were last on the card. Richard Henry and his opponent drew the very last slot of the evening. As she had promised, Louise had opted to stay at home. Billy Bob and his son sat through the fly weight, bantam weight and welter weight bouts. They watched as one of the fighters at the middle weight level knocked out his opponent in the first round with a savage right cross. The flattened young man remained unconscious for several minutes. Billy Bob just stared at the concrete floor and said a prayer for his son's safety.

Finally, it was time for Richard Henry to crawl into the ring. He was by the far the largest fighter of the entire night. He strode to the center of the canvas with a confident air. His opponent was waiting, along with the referee. There were no smiles tonight from the other fighter. Instead, he gave his opponent a death stare. The frightening look said everything. "I'm going to hurt you," it conveyed.

Richard Henry did not hear a word the referee said. He ambled back to his corner and heard the bell ring. He marched to the center of the ring with his arms down. His opponent approached him doing a classic bob and weave. Richard Henry suddenly stopped and remained stationary. Then he took his gloved right fist, raised it high into the air and crashed it down like a hammer directly on the top of his surprised opponent crew-cut head. The other fighter gave Richard Henry a quizzical look. Then, his eyes rolled back in his head. He sank to his knees. The young man remained motionless as the referee did a "9 count". Then the young black man arose. He looked at Richard Henry with surprise and respect. The next two minutes were the worst of Billy Bob's life. He watched as the muscular young man hit his son at least 40 times in 120 seconds. The final blow lifted Richard Henry nearly a foot off the canvas. He came back down and lay crumpled and unmoving. The ref quickly administered the final "10" count and the fight was over. Billy Bob rushed into the ring and sped to his son's side. Richard Henry looked up at his dad. He was smiling. His brain seemed intact.

"Well, at least I got in one good shot," he grinned.

Years later, the Heavyweight Champion of the World was asked by a reporter about the hardest blow he had ever taken in a fight.

"Yeah," the Champ replied, "It was at the Golden Gloves. This real tall white kid hit me right on the top of my head and nearly knocked me out. It was a real haymaker. No joke. I couldn't believe it. I heard he later became a ballet dancer or something like that." In fact, he did. But Richard

Luke 15: The Prodigal Son

Henry Fillmore always treasured his prodigal moment when he flattened the future Heavyweight Champion of the World with one punch.

THE PRODIGAL SON'S BROTHER TELLS ALL

Of course, I was mad. Wouldn't you be? My father always gave my younger brother more of everything—especially love and attention. I was the good kid. Since I am the oldest, I had to demonstrate total responsibility in every area. My dad expected me to work hard and be punctual and obedient. Meanwhile, the irresponsible kid sloughed off and never paid attention to the clock. He quickly figured out how to disappear for hours or even days. The old man would send me out to find his sorry butt. Of course, I knew where to look. The kid would either be drunk somewhere under a tree, lying with the town tramp or maybe both simultaneously. Oh, the little rounder used to get so mad when I ran him down. He gave me some lip on more than one occasion. Yet, I could not touch him. My father would have my head. The kid knew just how far he could stretch things with the old man.

When he asked my father for his share of the family estate, I was not surprised. He loved getting things first, ahead of me. I never sought any special favors from my father. I just kept my head down and did what was expected of me. I really do not know how to operate otherwise. Remember, I'm the good one. I figured my dad's money would not last very long. My brother is a spendthrift. He indulges himself by getting everything his heart desires. He also has no moral compass. Women are there for his pleasure. He doesn't respect himself so how can he respect anyone else?

I always figured the kid would come home when he lost everything. Sure enough, he did. The spoiled brat does not possess what it takes to live out on the street. What did surprise me was my father's reaction when he showed up. The old man fell all over himself in welcoming the worthless straggler with open arms. Killing the fatted calf? You must be kidding me! I never even got a skinny goat. Do I think my father took me for granted? Absolutely! When my kid brother went AWOL, I had to work twice as hard. My dad is not getting any younger either. He never said much about the slacker while he was out making a fool of himself. I do know my father was hurt when the kid left us both behind. But my dad never said one bad thing about him. I really wonder if I would have received the same consideration. Yes, I know my old man loves me. But there was something about an errant and lost kid that really touched his heart. My dad would stand at the kitchen window many days and just stare out at the fields. I think he had faith that one day his youngest son would come home. And, sure enough, he did.

How have things gone since the little dude came home? I sense a lot more gratitude and humility on his part. I notice that he treats my father with a respect that I never saw before. He also seems willing to work harder, especially on the things that once seemed beneath him. Surprisingly, the guy even treats me with a little more appreciation and consideration. He even asks for my opinion and advice. That never happened before. It is as if the world has become clearer since he was out wallowing with the hogs. Getting a higher vision is a good thing!

All in all, I'm glad that my brother came home. There was a definite hole in my dad's heart during his absence. It helps that my father is a forgiving person. He just never gave up on his youngest son. Would he do the same for me? Without a doubt, but then neither of us will ever have to find out.

THE PRODIGAL SON SITS DOWN FOR A PERSONAL INTERVIEW

Q. How does it feel to be famous for thousands of years?

A. I must be honest. It's much more than I would have ever expected when I was out there slopping the pigs.

Q. Yes, but most people cite your story as a cautionary tale. They say it shows what somebody should not do.

A. I guess you could look at it that way. I tend to believe that I provided a valuable life lesson that has endured over countless centuries. Not many people who have walked the earth can say as much.

Q. What do you regard as the premiere life lesson of your story?

A. Oh, there were many lessons. However, I believe one of the most important is "patience". Human beings are impatient souls. We want what we want when want it. I certainly did. I wanted my inheritance right then. I never liked to wait on anything. That was just the human part of me acting up, I guess.

The Prodigal Son Sits Down For A Personal Interview

Q. Did you expect your father to grant your request for your portion of the estate. Were you surprised?

A. Honestly, yes. There was no reason for him to do it. He should have known that giving me my portion early would create a rift in the family. Sure enough, it did. Then, when my father welcomed me back with such a show of affection, it caused the wound to grow even deeper with my older brother. I know my going and coming back were both painful for him. I regret that now. At the time, I could have cared less. I was not only impatient, I was also selfish. My life lesson involved learning how to turn away from ego gratification. I needed to learn some humility and I did. I had to take responsibility for my actions.

Q. What about the amoral way you squandered your inheritance?

A. It wasn't pretty. That involved my ego too. I kept telling myself that those women loved me for whom I am. What they loved was my money and attention. They were not as interested in me when I became penniless and started smelling like a hog. I never saw any of them again. It was another life lesson learned, with some pain attached.

Q. What were the takeaways from your experience as the Prodigal Son.

A. Again, there were so many. Number one is about the danger of pure selfishness. If I had just waited for my inheritance to arrive naturally, everyone would have been happier. But no, I had to have it now. So many bad decisions are made when the ego seizes control. Another thing I learned was about having respect for my father. He is such an amazing man. When I came sniveling home, he could have turned me away. No one would have blamed him, especially not my older brother. However, my dad welcomed me back with open arms and a forgiving heart. Can you understand how that made me feel? Nobody said: "I told you so." I felt loved, understood, and forgiven. Did I deserve it? Absolutely not!

Q. What would you tell someone else who was determined to follow your example as a Prodigal Son?

A. Think twice, and then think again. If that is the only way to learn your lesson, then go for it. Otherwise, stay where you are. Show some maturity. Take a good, long look at yourself. Tell the ego to take a hike. You will be glad you did. Nobody deserves to find themselves rolling with the hogs.

THE PRODIGAL SON'S FATHER EXPLAINS EVERYTHING

"I know my actions confused many people. Why was I so eager to welcome back my youngest son, the "Prodigal"? Why did I forgive the squandering of his inheritance on foolish things? What about putting the finest robes on someone who disrespected his family? Why did I seemingly snub his older and more responsible brother? I acknowledge there are many questions about the way I handled everything. I understand the confusion. My own heart and mind were conflicted about the situation. That is the way life sometimes unfolds. I think there are many "grey" areas when it comes to family relations. No one can really know the human heart.

Let's start at the beginning. Why did I agree to say "yes" when my son asked for his inheritance early? I knew it was a bad idea. I could have predicted the outcome. However, I asked myself: "Who am I to stand in the way of a life lesson someone needs to learn?" My youngest boy would have received his half of my estate at some point. If he was intent on receiving it early, maybe he needed to learn one of his lessons now. Of course, he showed "impatience" with his request. Human beings hate to wait on

The Prodigal Son's Father Explains Everything

anything. The younger generation can be quite shortsighted. I am certain my son never envisioned that he would end up broke and feeding the hogs. It probably never entered his mind about negative consequences.

Of course, I worried that my older son would think that I took him for granted. In some ways, I did. He was always so responsible. He never disappointed me in any way. When his younger brother disappeared, it put an even greater responsibility on him. He never complained or tried to shirk his duties. I showed my appreciation, but I probably could have done more. I guess human nature always makes us pine for what is missing in our lives. My youngest son's prodigal behavior falls into that category. I missed him every day that he was gone.

I know how it must have looked when I fell all over my boy when he turned up so unexpectedly. I had always yearned for his return. But when it happened, I was surprised. My happiness was beyond description. It was as though the hole in my heart healed in one second. I probably went a little bit overboard, with the fatted calf and all. When my oldest son showed up mad, I should have been more sensitive to his feelings. If I could do it over again, I would handle things better. More than likely, that son still holds a grudge against his younger brother. He abandoned his family for the fast life. I hope my older son can find forgiveness for both me and the Prodigal. I hope everybody understands that I

Luke 15: The Prodigal Son

love each son equally. I am trying to watch myself in playing favorites.

Children should try and understand how imperfect we dads and moms are when applying our parenting skills. We just do the best we can at the time. Nobody handed us a rule book before the babies arrived. Everything was handed down verbally from one generation to the next. But what may have worked in one parent/child relationship can fail miserably in another. I could have told my youngest son to avoid fast women when he left home. Would he have listened? Of course not. It would have been in one ear and out the other. He had to experience those hard lessons at his own pace. Will he remember those bad times in future situations? One can only hope. In the meantime, all I can do is forgive him and love both of my sons equally. I hope God gives me the wisdom and strength to do just that."

UNDERSTANDING THE PRODIGAL IN YOUR LIFE

Most people will probably have to deal with prodigal behavior from somebody sooner or later. Human nature dictates that the status quo must be tested and probed. What goes into launching an individual on the prodigal path? Here are specific considerations when evaluating the potential or actual prodigal in your life:

(1) **CONTROL ISSUES**—Almost everybody strives to exert control over things that impact their lives. When people feel constrained or controlled by others, they often seek relief. That may include leaving the parental home, abandoning a relationship or quitting a job or formal schooling. Prodigals often seek control of their own decisions and life choices.

(2) **SEEKING A DIFFERENT WAY OF LIFE**—Children are usually born into a particular family that functions with already established rules and procedures. Family members expect acceptance and compliance by anyone joining the family. These rules can also apply to in-laws and extended family. Someone pushing

back against conforming to the structure of a family, relationship or job becomes a possible candidate for prodigal behavior.

(3) **EGO CENTERED ORIENTATION**— Many prodigals exhibit self-centeredness. Being the center of their own personal universe ranks ahead of anything else. How other people may experience them or be hurt by their decisions has no impact. They expect others to adjust expectations or opinions. Ego-centered prodigals are often triggered by drug and alcohol issues.

(4) **IMPATIENCE**—Prodigals tend to be impatient. They have little interest in waiting their turn or standing in line. They seek shortcuts. Prodigals want what they want right now, not in the future. They carry a stopwatch, not a calendar. Reason, logic or talking things out has no appeal. The Prodigal is only interested in immediate action and the sooner the better.

(5) **INFLEXIBILITY**—Just as nobody has ever won a fact-based argument with an addict, prodigals are usually immune to rationality. Unless it conforms to their own often unique conclusions, they have no interest in counterarguments. Trying to deal logically with the prodigal mind can be an exercise in futility.

Luke 15: The Prodigal Son

HOW TO DEAL WITH THE PRODIGAL MINDSET

If someone in your life is engaging in prodigal thoughts or actions, here are some options to consider:

(1) **KEEP THE FOCUS ON WHAT YOU CAN CONTROL**—Most recovery programs, such as Alcoholics Anonymous and Al-Anon Family Groups recommend The Serenity Prayer: "God grant me the serenity to accept the things I cannot change, courage to change the things I can and the wisdom to know the difference." Obsessing about someone else's behavior is usually unproductive. A focus on practicing self-care, taking responsibility for our own behavior, and turning within to a Higher Power for comfort and guidance offers better outcomes.

(2) **"DISLIKE THE SIN, LOVE THE SINNER"**—It is easy to find fault with the words or actions of people we care about. Withholding your love as a form of punishment is not a good plan. Love acts as the healing factor when and if the prodigal phase ends. In the parable of "The Prodigal Son", the father kept his love alive. When

the son returned, he was able to summon up the unconditional love that remained intact.

(3) **PRACTICE ONGOING FORGIVENESS FOR EVERYONE**—Living in a state of continuous forgiveness brings peace, serenity and contentment. Prodigals need people in their lives who know how to forgive. Life itself is rife with daily opportunities for forgiveness. Maintaining a forgiving attitude may not be easy. However, refusing to release grudges can wreck anyone's emotional well-being. Maybe you cannot forget, but you can forgive. Extending a pardon to someone who wronged you can bring relief for everyone involved.

(4) **TAKE OFF THE JUDGE'S BLACK ROBE**—"Judge not, least you be judged" is one of Jesus' wisest statements from "The Sermon on the Mount". Human beings love to judge people and situations. Everyone has experienced judgement. It is never a pleasant experience. No one can know the complete facts about anyone or anything, yet people feel free to render a judgement. This may come as a surprise to some, but we are not required

to have an opinion about everything. "You may be right" or "That's one way to look at it" are two good neutral responses whenever judgements start to fly. Even opinions about prodigal behavior can be wrong. Radical decisions and actions sometimes turn out better than expected. What seems like a negative "Life Lesson" may produce unexpected and positive results in the long run.

(5) **BEHOLD THE HOLY SPIRIT IN EVERYONE, INCLUDING THE PRODIGAL**—We are all God's beloved children. That includes the Prodigal in your life. He or she was created perfectly in God's image and likeness. God already loves the Prodigal more than you ever could. Picture this person surrounded by God's Light, enfolded in God's Love, protected by God's Presence and watched over by the Spirit of God and the angels of Heaven. Trust that all is proceeding in Divine Order.

THE TWELVE GIFTS OF THE PRODIGAL SON PARABLE

1. **LOYALTY**—Although the older son plays a lesser role in this parable, he demonstrated loyalty to his father. He acted in a responsible manner after the Prodigal left home. Throughout the time of the Prodigal Son's absence, the other brother remained at home and fulfilled his family duties. In the parable, his loyal actions seem to go unrewarded. The oldest son felt slighted by his father's warm welcome of the lost son. Still, loyalty represents a valuable gift to anyone fortunate enough to receive it.

2. **UNCONDITIONAL FORGIVENESS**—The Prodigal Son's father demonstrated unconditional forgiveness. He did not say "I told you so!" or express negative judgment about his youngest son's behavior. Instead, the Prodigal is welcomed home with parental relief and open arms. The lost child has been recovered. That is enough for the happy father.

3. **HOPE**—The Prodigal's father never lost hope. Even though bad decisions and negative behavior were evident, the father did not give up on his wayward son. This parable urges us to keep expecting a positive outcome despite outer appearances. In the end, the father's attitude was rewarded.

4. **LOVE**—A parent's love for their children represents a powerful and lasting emotion. Love for a lost child supersedes almost anything else. For the Prodigal Son's father, the reaction to his son's return was proof of a parent's deep and lasting affection.

5. **GENEROSITY**—Obviously, the father did not approve of the Prodigal's life choices and errant behavior. However, he chose to react with generosity both before and after the Prodigal leaving home. The father honored the Prodigal's request for his inheritance early, even though he could have anticipated the outcome. The father's generosity of spirit was especially evident when the prodigal returned home broke and humbled.

6. **UNDERSTANDING**—Parents often do not understand their children and vice versa. Family misunderstandings often last a lifetime. Had the Prodigal Son not

returned home, the relationship with his father probably would not have been restored. Mending a severed relationship demands high levels of understanding on everyone's part. Before anything positive can occur, both parties must be open to healing deep wounds.

7. **PERSEVERANCE**—The father in this timeless parable demonstrated perseverance. He kept hoping for his son's return. If we will keep believing in God's miracles, our own perseverance may someday be rewarded. Never giving up on someone demands extraordinary faith and perseverance.

8. **PATIENCE**—Remaining patient with prodigal behavior may be too great a challenge for many. Yet allowing the prodigal enough time to experience outcomes can have positive results, as demonstrated in this timeless parable. Most "Life Lessons" are not learned overnight. Practicing patience during stressful times requires bottomless faith and prayerful belief. This is especially difficult in the parent-child relationship.

9. **WISDOM**—The Prodigal Son's father displayed considerable wisdom. He honored the request by the son for his share of the family estate. The father trusted in

the eventual outcome. His wise handling of a tricky situation resulted in the son's return. The older son disagreed with his father offering a warm welcome to the Prodigal. The father did display some awareness in his response, reassuring the eldest son of his important place in the family.

10. **KINDNESS**—The Prodigal Son's father showed a high degree of kindness for his youngest child. He must have realized that the Prodigal was hurting. defeated and vulnerable. Rather than rub the son's nose in his mistakes, the father treated him with kindness and compassion. Everyone has a time when they need understanding. Stay on the alert for the people in your life that may require extra kindness and attention.

11. **MERCY**—When the humbled Prodigal came groveling home, he did not expect his father's mercy. However, he also could not have anticipated the warmth, love, and forgiveness shown toward him. The father could have displayed a merciless attitude towards his wayward son. Yet he turned away from any harsh judgment and granted mercy instead. We all have opportunities to show mercy toward others as we navigate our life journey. Always choose mercy over condemnation.

Luke 15: The Prodigal Son

11. GRACE—God's Grace was present throughout this famous parable. Although the Prodigal Son engaged in wasteful and even dangerous behavior, he was protected by God until he could change his mind and return home. It was through divine Grace that the father welcomed him back with an open heart and unconditional love. Love is a visible form of Grace. This parable offers a joyful ending for both father and son. Without God's Grace, that would have been an impossible outcome.

A FINAL THOUGHT: WHY WE ARE ALL PRODIGALS

The dictionary defines a prodigal as "someone who spends money recklessly". In that sense, all of us probably qualify as prodigals. Most everybody has spent money unwisely. In a sense, wasting our money on unwise investments, gambling, pursuit of passing fads or pleasure seeking often becomes how we learn "life lessons". Blowing hard earned cash often sets up valuable consequences. In the "Prodigal Son" parable, the youngest son squandered his inheritance. That led to his job feeding the hogs. Without his reckless spending, the Prodigal might never have realized the intrinsic value of family. If we were to review how we spent our own money in the past, some valuable life lessons might be revealed. Patterns, both positive and negative, could emerge and provide clarity. Spending money on anything is a clue to our priorities. Have our expenditures produced positive or negative results for ourselves and others? Learning life's lessons is a crucial part of our spiritual journey. How we allocate our money can determine the outcome of our lives. As with the Prodigal Son, it could well be the key element in our destiny. Will how we use our money be a blessing or a curse? As with everything else, God gives us the free

A Final Thought: Why We Are All Prodigals

will to choose. Revisiting the parable of The Prodigal Son, we can gain knowledge and wisdom that can inform, enlighten and bless us.

ABOUT THE AUTHOR

Rev. Allen C. Liles is an ordained minister and creator of the Classic Bible Chapter Series. Before entering the ministry, he served as Vice-President of Public Relations for the 7-Eleven stores in Dallas, Texas and Community Relations Manager for the McLane Company in Temple, Texas. For more information, please visit https://classicbiblechapters.com.

BOOKS BY ALLEN C. LILES

DANIEL 6/SURVIVING THE LION'S DEN

EXODUS 20/THE TEN COMMANDMENTS

EPHESIANS 6/PUTTING ON THE WHOLE ARMOR OF GOD

JOHN 14/THE MOST IMPORTANT CHAPTER IN THE NEW TESTAMENT

FINDING YOUR COMPANY'S SPIRITUAL PURPOSE

SITTING WITH GOD/MEDITATING FOR GOD'S DIVINE GUIDANCE/A YEAR OF SPIRITUAL GROWTH

THE 7 PUZZLES OF LIFE/GOD'S PLAN TO SAVE THE WORLD

THE FOREVER PENNY/HOW OUR LOVED ONES STAY CONNECTED AFTER DEATH

OH THANK HEAVEN/THE STORY OF THE SOUTHLAND CORPORATION

Books by Allen C. Liles at Smashwords.com

The Forever Penny: How Our Loved Ones Stay Connected After Death
https://www.smashwords.com/books/view/839864

The Book of Ethan/God Confronts Teen Suicide
https://www.smashwords.com/books/view/647665

The Book of Floyd/God Transforms a Racist
https://www.smashwords.com/books/view/615914

The Book of Celeste
https://www.smashwords.com/books/view/593856

E-Spiritual Rehab/28 Online Days to Healing Your Spirit
https://www.smashwords.com/books/view/481978

Friends of Jesus
https://www.smashwords.com/books/view/455617

The 12 Promises of Heaven
https://www.smashwords.com/books/view/444920

www.ingramcontent.com/pod-product-compliance
Lightning Source LLC
Chambersburg PA
CBHW062141280426
43673CB00072B/88